T.A.S.K. Media presents

Where's
My
Daddy?

Jamiyl Samuels & Tracy-Ann Samuels

Illustrated by : INDOS Studio

Where's My Daddy?

For more information, please contact:
The Amazingly Sensational Kids
www.TheAmazinglySensationalKids.com
ISBN -13: 978-1-7378108-0-3

DISCLAIMER

"Where's My Daddy?" is part one of a book series that touches on a subject that may bring about unresolved feelings of abandonment, pain, and anger in some readers. It is not intended to offend but spark the tough conversation that is so often suppressed. Regardless of if the story is relatable to you or your family, children are our future leaders, scholars, and, most importantly, parents and they deserve transparency no matter their age.

At the conclusion of the book there is a worksheet that asks universal questions about the story to find out how your child(ren) can relate to the character of Jaylen and their thoughts on how they would respond in her situation.

A word from Jamiyl Samuels:

This children's book is based on a true story:

My abandonment by my father when I was a ten-year old boy devastated me. For years I carried the hurt, pain, anger and trauma of not having the person I looked up to in my life. When I became a dad, I was determined not to follow in my father's footsteps. I thought I was a good father because I was present. I was breaking the cycle of the 'deadbeat dad' because I did not leave my children. It was only recently that I re alized, despite writing my feelings out in my debut book "Pass The Torch: How A Young Black Father Challenges The Deadbeat Dad Stereotype", I was still broken and stuck in my trauma of unresolved feelings. Even though I was in the same home, I wasn't actively involved in my children's lives. I learned I did not value the things my dad did with me because I thought he would never leave.

This book is written with the express purpose to have the tough conversation about the traumas that may linger and grow to affect young Black men and women. A pain that is usually left unaddressed and carries into a relationship and could damage the bond with the next generation.

Jaylen James is me; she is you, she is your mother, your father. It is important that we not only praise the great Black Fathers and phenomenal Black Women and Mothers but speak on the generational curses they are working to break and where it comes from. While some men don't care to be a father, we are here to glorify the ones who do. This book series is the conversation I wish I had.

DEDICATION

To all the boys and girls who came from broken homes who grew to be strong mothers and fathers. Make sure to address any residual feelings so you can be the best parent to your child.

Little Jaylen James loved her Daddy.
Every day before he would leave for work, he would poke his head into her room.
"Hey, hey, JJ!"
Hearing her Daddy's call always put a smile on her face.

Her Daddy taught her to play sports like soccer and softball.
Whenever Daddy received his weekly paycheck, he brought home a special treat of nuggets and fries with her favorite sweet and sour sauce.

Jaylen waited up for her Daddy to come home from work every night.
Lately, Daddy would come home later and later in the evening.

This led to a lot of mean words between Mommy and Daddy.
This made Jaylen sad.
Over the next few days Jaylen fell asleep each night before Daddy came home

One day, with tears in her eyes, Jaylen sat down next to her Daddy. "Are you going to leave Mommy?" she asked
"No," Daddy said.
A week later Jaylen woke up to find Daddy driving away from home.

Days and weeks went by, but Daddy never came home.
Where did Daddy go?
Jaylen was angry. She did not understand why her
Daddy would leave after saying that he wouldn't.

Mama James, Jaylen's Grandma, came to visit to check on her. She saw how sad her granddaughter was.
"What's the matter, baby?"
Jaylen knew Mama James was Daddy's mommy so whenever she came by, she would ask her:
"Where's My Daddy?"

Mama James sat next to Jaylen and gave her a big hug. "Your Daddy made a mistake," she said.
"Did he leave because of me?" Jaylen asked with tears in her eyes.
"Ofcourse not," Grandma began. "It is not your fault."
Jaylen put her head down.
"Where's My Daddy?"

Mama James took a deep breath. "Daddy needs time to think," she began. "Just know he loves you very much."
Jaylen stands up "No he doesn't!"
"Why would you say that?" Mama James continued.
"Because he would have come back like he always does, and he didn't!"
Mama James sighs.

"Sometimes grownups live apart when they do not agree on everything," Mama James said "I pray your Mommy and Daddy can come together and work out their problems." Jaylen felt a little better, but still missed her Daddy terribly.

One day Jaylen came home from school and was shocked to hear someone speaking that sounded just like her Daddy.
She slowly peaked around the corner and saw Grandma sitting in the living room. There was nobody else around.

"You both have to do better," she heard Grandma say. "You have a little girl to think about."
Jaylen began to move closer and saw that Mama James was on the phone.

"Where's my Daddy?" Jaylen asked confused.
Mama James slowly handed her the phone.
Jaylen put the phone to her ear.
"Hey hey, JJ!"

Where's My Daddy ? Questions

1 – What is happening in the story?
2 – How does Jaylen change from beginning to the end?
3 – How would you feel if you were Jaylen?
4 – What would you say to Jaylen?
5 – What would you say to her Daddy?

Draw a picture of yourself and your Daddy in the space below:

HELPING CHILDREN WITH AN ABSENT PARENT

Prepare yourself – this is a hard conversation to have for anyone.

Take a deep breath – it's a lot to take in.

Give yourself a moment – if you're not ready to share, take your time.

Allow your child(ren) to ask questions in a safe space without any judgement.

Validate their feelings.

Let them know they are not to blame.

Tell the facts about what happened in an age-appropriate manner.

Avoid bashing the absentee parent.

Share good memories about the absentee parent.

If you need help, reach out to a family member, pastor, or counselor.

JAMIYL SAMUELS is the founder of W.R.E.a.C Havoc Enterprises and co-founder of The Amazingly Sensational Kids (T.A.S.K.) media group, a company seeks to educate and entertain through the creation of informed written content, film, music, public speaking, and other media platforms. He began his college career as a Theater major at Morgan State University in 1996, but ultimately graduated with a Bachelor's degree in English and a Master's degree in Media Arts with a concentration in screenwriting from Long Island University in Brooklyn, New York. His ultimate goal is to expand the W.R.E.a.C. Havoc and T.A.S.K. brands worldwide. He is currently working on various projects related to the The Amazingly Awesome Amani series and other works based on the importance of fatherhood.

TRACY-ANN SAMUELS is the co-owner and chief operating officer of W.R.E.a.C Havoc Enterprises and The Amazingly Sensational Kids (T.A.S.K.) media group. She serves as an ambassador for Autism Speaks. She earned her Bachelor's degree in Psychology from Rutgers University and her Master's degree in Social Work from New York University. She has over 20 years of experience in the Social Services field. As a Senior Advisor at New York City Administration for Children's Services, she works with children who are Developmentally Delayed, Seriously Emotionally Disturbed, and Medically Fragile.
Her ultimate goal is to assist at-risk children and their families, counsel couples through relationship and/or marital issues, and make an impact in her community by educating parents about the resources available for children and adults with special needs.
The couple resides in New York with their two children.

www.ingramcontent.com/pod-product-compliance
Lightning Source LLC
Chambersburg PA
CBHW040245100426

42811CB00011B/1153